VOLUME ONE

Recital Winners

COMPILED AND EDITED BY
Carole L. Bigler and Valery Lloyd-Watts

CONTENTS

A recording of the repertoire in this volume is available from Alfred on CD (#11718). Expressively performed by concert artist Valery Lloyd-Watts, the recording enables pianists to enjoy the music and accelerate the learning process. When pianists hear this exciting, impressive music, they will want to learn it.

Piano photograph: courtesy of Yamaha Corporation of America
Art direction: Ted Engelbart   Cover design: Trish Meyer
Music engraving: Scores International

FOREWORD

"How can I motivate this piano student?" is one of the most frequently asked questions we hear from teachers and parents. After many years of teaching experience, we are pleased to offer some help with the answer.

Pianists of any age are motivated by music they like and music they can play. The repertoire in this compilation satisfies both requirements. The pieces were chosen because they appeal to the showmanship in students and because they are accessible to pianists at the early intermediate through late intermediate levels.

Some pieces are short, making it possible to learn them quickly. Many of them have either repeated or parallel passages, decreasing the learning time even more. Because these pieces are easily learned, completing them creates a feeling of accomplishment. Less experienced pianists can feel and sound like virtuosos.

This collection includes music from all eras. Each piece incorporates a particular technique such as glissando, hand crossings, full chords and/or dramatic leaps, making each of them impressive and fun to play. Arranged in approximate order of difficulty, they may be used as recital "winners," supplementary repertoire or as motivators to re-inspire a student.

These pieces have received enthusiastic responses. Many of our students have taken the initiative to learn the music on their own. Even more exciting to us is the obvious pleasure they experience as they practice and perform these **Recital Winners**!

Carole L. Bigler and Valery Lloyd-Watts

Grand Waltz

Muzio Clementi
(1752–1832)

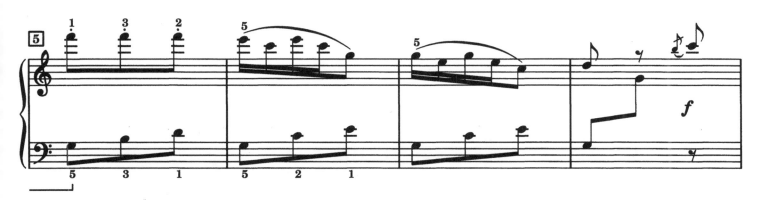

Sonata in C Major

Domenico Scarlatti (1685–1757)
K. 95; L. 358

Waltz in D Major

from *Letzte Walzer* (Last Waltzes), D. 146

Franz Schubert (1797–1828)
Op. 127, No. 1

Fine

D. C. al Fine

The Pearls

Friedrich Burgmüller (1806–1874)
Op. 109, No. 2

* The 32nd notes are printed in small type to indicate that they must be played softly
  to distinguish them from the melody notes.

Waltz in A Minor

Frédéric Chopin (1810–1849)
Posthumous

Allegretto (♩ = 96)

Novelette

Dmitri Kabalevsky (1904–1987)
Op. 27, No. 25

Flying Leaves

Carl Kölling (1831–1914)
Op. 147, No. 2

Waltz in A-flat Major

Johannes Brahms (1833–1897)
Op. 39, No. 15

*Ornamental notes are played before the beat.

Prelude in C Minor

à son ami J. C. Kessler

Frédéric Chopin (1810–1849)
Op. 28, No. 20

Tarantella

Albert Pieczonka

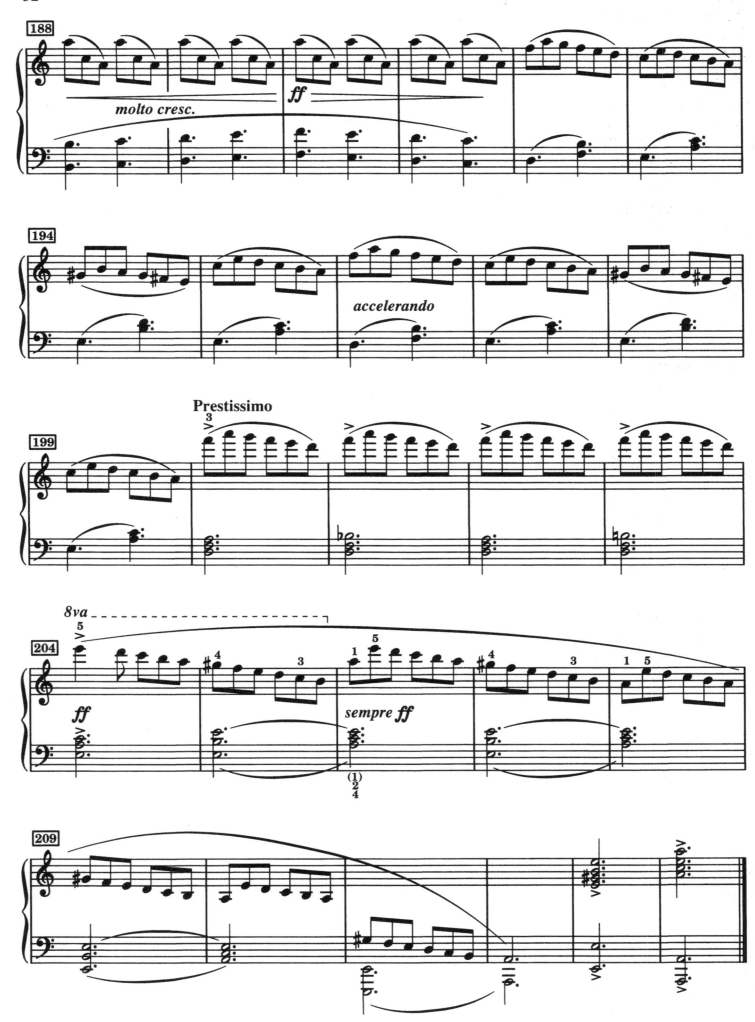